Key Concept Activity Lab Workbook

Martha Haehl
Maple Woods Community College

James M. Sullivan
Massachusetts Bay Community College

Introductory
Algebra

K. Elayn Martin-Gay
University of New Orleans

Prentice
Hall

PRENTICE HALL, Upper Saddle River, NJ 07458

Director of Product Development: *Christine B. Hoag*
Development Editor: *Elaine Page*
Production Editor: *Barbara A. Till*
Supplement Cover Design: *Maureen Eide*
Special Projects Manager: *Barbara A. Murray*
Manufacturing Buyer: *Alan Fischer*

Printed in the United States of America

10 9 8 7 6 5 4

0-13-010400-0

Prentice-Hall International (UK) Limited, *London*
Prentice-Hall of Australia Pty. Limited, *Sydney*
Prentice-Hall Canada, Inc., *Toronto*
Prentice-Hall Hispanoamericana, S.A., *Mexico*
Prentice-Hall of India Private Limited, *New Delhi*
Prentice-Hall of Japan, Inc., *Tokyo*
Pearson Education Asia Pte., Ltd., *Singapore*
Editora Prentice-Hall do Brasil, Ltda., *Rio de Janeiro*

Table of Contents

Interactive Math Objective Chart—Linking the Key Concept Exercises to Objectives

Each of the exercises in the Key Concept Activity Lab Workbook are supported by Objectives within Interactive Math. These Objectives and topics are listed in the chart below:

Key Concept Activity	Topics and Objectives Covered			
	Extension	Conceptual	Group	Open Environment
Room to Grow (Chapter 1) pp. 1-10	1.1.3, 1.2.1, 1.2.2, 1.2.3, 1.3.2, 1.3.3, 1.7.1 symbols, fractions, exponents, operations on real numbers	1.1.3, 1.2.2, 1.3.2, 1.3.3, 1.4.1, 1.4.2, 1.4.3, 1.4.4, 1.5.1, 1.6.1, 1.6.2, 1.6.3, 1.6.4, 1.7.1 symbols, fractions, exponents, variables, operations on real numbers	1.1.2, 1.1.3, 1.3.3, 1.4.1, 1.4.2, 1.4.3, 1.4.4, 1.5.1, 1.5.3, 1.6.1, 1.6.2, 1.6.3, 1.6.4, 1.7.1, 1.7.2, 1.9.1 symbols, exponents, variables, operations on real numbers, interpreting graphs	1.1.2, 1.2.1, 1.2.2, 1.3.1, 1.3.2, 1.3.3, 1.4.1, 1.4.2, 1.4.3, 1.4.4, 1.7.1, 1.7.2 symbols, fractions, exponents, operations on real numbers
A Chill in the Air (Chapter 2) pp. 11-20	2.4.2, 2.6.2, 1.9.1, 2.9.2, 2.9.3, 2.9.5 solving linear equations, formulas, problem solving, interpreting graphs, linear inequalities	2.4.2, 2.6.2, 1.9.1, 2.9.2, 2.9.3, 2.9.5 solving linear equations, formulas, problem solving, intepreting graphs, linear inequalities	2.5.1, 2.6.1, 2.6.2, 2.8.4 problem solving, formulas	2.5.1, 2.6.1, 2.6.2, 1.5.1, 1.6.1, 1.7.1 problem solving, formulas, operations on real numbers
The Race (Chapter 3) pp. 21-30	2.8.2, 2.4.1 problem solving, solving linear equations	3.1.1, 3.1.2, 3.1.4, 3.3.1, 3.3.2, 3.3.3, 3.4.1 rectangular coordinate system, ordered pairs, plotting points, intercepts, slope	2.8.4, 3.4.1, 2.6.1, 2.6.2 problem solving, formulas, slope	2.8.4, 3.1.1, 3.1.2, 3.1.4, 3.3.1, 3.3.2, 3.3.3, 3.4.1, 1.9.2 problem solving, rectangular coordinate system, ordered pairs, plotting points, intercepts, slope, interpreting graphs
Information Skyway (Chapter 4) pp. 31-40	4.1.1, 4.5.2, 4.5.3, 4.5.4, 2.8.2, 2.6.2 formulas, problem solving, exponents, scientific notation	2.6.2, 2.8.2, 4.1.1, 4.5.2, 4.5.3, 4.5.4 formulas, problem solving, exponents, scientific notation	4.2.1, 4.2.2, 4.2.3, 4.2.4, 1.9.1, 4.5.3 interpreting graphs, adding and subtracting polynomials, scientific notation	4.4.3, 2.8.2 formulas, problem solving, sum and difference of two terms
More Space for Bruin (Chapter 5) pp. 41-50	5.6.1, 5.6.2, 5.3.1, 5.3.2, 5.3.3, 5.3.4, 5.7.1 factoring trinomials, solving quadratic equations by factoring, problem solving with quadratic equations	5.6.1, 5.6.2, 5.6.3, 5.3.1, 5.3.2, 5.3.3, 5.3.4, 5.7.1, 3.1.1, 3.1.2 factoring trinomials, rectangular coordinate system, ordered pairs, plotting points, solving quadratic equations, problem solving	5.7.1 quadratic equations and problem solving	5.6.1, 5.6.2, 5.3.1, 5.3.2, 5.3.3, 5.3.4, 5.7.1, 3.1.1, 3.1.2 rectangular coordinate system, plotting ordered pairs, factoring trinomials, solving quadratic equations, problem solving

Key Concept Activity	Topics and Objectives Covered			
	Extension	**Conceptual**	**Group**	**Open Environment**
Affording a Car (Chapter 6) pp. 51-60	2.8.4, 6.8.1, 6.1.1, 6.6.1, 6.6.2, 6.6.3 problem solving, simplifying rational expressions, solving equations with rational expressions,	6.7.1, 6.7.2, 6.7.3, 6.7.4 ratio, proportions	6.8.1, 6.6.1, 6.6.2, 6.6.3, 2.8.2 rational equations, problem solving, solving equations with rational expressions	6.1.1, 6.8.1, 6.6.1, 6.6.2, 6.6.3, 3.1.1, 3.1.2 rectangular coordinate system, plotting ordered pairs, solving equations with rational expressions, problem solving and rational equations
Chain Reaction (Chapter 7) pp. 61-70	7.4.1, 7.4.2, 7.4.3, 7.4.4 functions and function notation	6.7.1, 6.7.2, 6.7.3, 6.7.4, 4.5.3, 7.2.4 ratio, proportions, scientific notation, point-slope form	3.1.1, 3.1.2, 3.4.1, 7.1.1, 7.1.3, 7.1.4 rectangular coordinate system, plotting ordered pairs, slope, slope-intercept form	7.1.4, 7.4.4, 3.1.2, 3.4.1, 7.1.1 slope-intercept form, functions, plotting ordered pairs, slope
Check, Please (Chapter 8) pp. 71-84	8.4.1, 8.2.1 solving systems of equations by substitution, problem solving with systems	8.1.1, 8.1.2, 8.1.3, 8.4.1 solving systems by graphing, problem solving with systems	8.1.1, 8.2.1, 8.3.1, 8.4.1 solving systems by graphing, substitution, and addition, problem solving with systems	8.1.1, 8.1.2, 8.2.1, 8.4.1 solving systems by graphing and substitution, problem solving with systems
Mysteries of the Past (Chapter 9) pp. 85-94	9.6.3, 9.6.1, 2.5.1, 2.6.1, 6.8.1 formulas, rational equations, radical equations and problem solving	9.6.1, 9.6.2, 9.6.3, 3.1.2, 7.4.4 radical equations and problem solving, plotting points, function notation	9.6.3, 9.6.1, 2.5.1, 2.6.1, 2.6.2 formulas, radical equations and problem solving	9.6.3, 2.5.1, 2.6.1 formulas, radical equations and problem solving
Reaching the Peak (Chapter 10) pp. 95-106	2.5.1, 2.6.1, 10.4.1, 10.6.1, 10.6.2, 10.6.3, 10.6.4, 7.4.4, 8.2.1 problem solving, formulas, functions, solving systems by substitution, graphing quadratic equations	2.5.1, 2.6.1, 10.4.1, 10.6.1, 10.6.2, 10.6.3, 10.6.4, 10.3.1 problem solving, formulas, solving quadratic equations by quadratic formula, methods for solving quadratic equations, graphing quadratic equations	2.5.1, 10.3.1, 8.2.1, 10.4.1, 10.6.2 problem solving, quadratic equations solved by quadratic formula, methods for solving quadratic equations, graphing quadratic equations, solving systems by substitution	10.6.2, 10.6.2, 10.6.3, 10.6.4, 10.3.1, 10.4.1, 2.5.1, 8.2.1 problem solving, solving systems by substitution, graphing quadratic equations, solving quadratic equations by quadratic formula, methods for solving quadratic equations

Chapter 1—Review of Real Numbers
Key Concept Activity #1: Room to Grow

1.   Group Activity—Measure Your Classroom

2.   Conceptual Exercise—Fencing In Your Garden

3.   Open Environment Activity—Circles and Squares

4.   Extension Exercise—A Recipe for Soil Replacement

1. Group Activity—Measure Your Classroom

Work with your group members to measure your classroom. To ensure accuracy, it is helpful for two people to do the measuring while a third person records the measurements. Show all of your computations as you answer the following questions.

a. What is the height from floor to ceiling?

_____

b. How many square feet of floor space does your classroom have?

_____

c. How many feet of baseboard trim would it (or does it) take to go around the room?

_____

d. Recall that 1 yard = 3 feet and that a square yard is a square that measures 1 yard by one yard. On the grid below, draw a representation for 1 foot, 1 yard, 1 square foot, and 1 square yard. Label each drawing. Let 1 unit segment on the grid represent 1 foot and 1 square represent 1 square foot.

☐ 1 square foot

— 1 foot

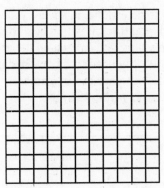

Use your notes on the drawing to make the following conversions.

1 square yard = _____ square feet   1 square foot = _____ square yard

e. Using the grid below, draw the floor space in your classroom. Let one unit segment on the grid represent 1 foot in your classroom and one square on the grid represent 1 square foot. Compare your drawing with those of your group members to check for accuracy.

f. Write a brief memo to your school asking to have new carpet installed in the classroom. Using the prices below, include the total cost for your request.
- carpet – $15.35 per square yard
- carpet pad – $1.75 per square yard
- installation fee – $2.15 per square yard
- delivery fee – $45.00

Refer to your drawing in part *e* to determine, in square yards, the floor space of your room. In your request, state how much you think it would cost to carpet the classroom. Round your answer to the nearest cent. Show how you calculated the amount of carpet needed and the cost. Explain why you would probably need to buy more carpet than the exact number of square yards in the room. Work with your group members to compare calculations and opinions. Share your group's memo with other groups in your class.

_____

_____

_____

_____

_____

2. Conceptual Exercise—Fencing In Your Garden

Suppose you want to build a fence around the garden that you designed in Key Concept Activity #1: Room to Grow. You have the money to buy 60 feet of fencing material. This exercise will help you determine the shape of the largest fenced-in garden possible.

The <u>area</u> of a rectangle is computed by multiplying the length times the width. Area is two-dimensional and is measured in square units. The <u>perimeter</u> of a rectangle is the length around the rectangle. Therefore, the perimeter of a rectangular garden plot is equal to how long the fence is around the entire garden.

a. For each of the following widths, find the length and area of the garden if the garden is enclosed with 60 feet of fencing. *Hint:* If the perimeter is 60 feet, then the length is 30 feet minus the width.

Width in Feet	Length in Feet (30 − width)	Check that Perimeter is 60 Feet (2 • width + 2 • length)	Area in Square Feet (length • width)
11			
12			
13			
14			
15			
16			
17			

b. What dimensions (length by width) give the rectangle of greatest area? _____

c. What is the name of the special shape of the rectangle of greatest area? _____

d. After reviewing the data in part *b*, suppose you decide that you would like more garden area, but you do not want to buy more fencing material. One way to accomplish this is to reposition your garden plot so that the side of your house forms one side of the garden and the fencing forms the other three sides. Draw a diagram to show how the house and fence will form the sides of the garden.

e. When one side of the garden is against the house, the 60 feet of fencing can be used to form the remaining three sides. Notice from the drawing that two of the fenced sides are the same length. In the table below, fill in the second and third columns.

Width in Feet	Length in Feet (60 − 2 • width)	Area in Square Feet (length • width)
12	60 - 2(12) =	
13	60 - 2(13) =	
14	60 - 2(14) =	
15	60 - 2(15) =	
16	60 - 2(16) =	

3. Open Environment Activity—Circles and Squares

Would you get more or less garden space if a 60-foot fence surrounded a circular garden instead of a square garden? The formula for the area A of a circle with circumference C is $A = \dfrac{C^2}{4\pi}$.

To use this formula for a circle with a circumference of 60 feet, calculate the following:

$$\frac{60^2}{4\pi}$$

Recall that π (pi) is an irrational number. In computations, 3.14, 3.1416, and $3\frac{1}{7}$ are frequently used as approximations for π. To get a more accurate approximation (to more decimal places), use the π key on your calculator tool.

a. What approximation does your calculator tool give for π? _____

b. Compute the arithmetic expression $\dfrac{60^2}{4\pi}$ on the calculator tool with the following keystrokes:

$$\boxed{(}\;\boxed{60}\;\boxed{\wedge}\;\boxed{2}\;\boxed{)}\;\boxed{\div}\;\boxed{(}\;\boxed{4}\;\boxed{\times}\;\boxed{\pi}\;\boxed{)}\;\boxed{\text{ENTER}}$$

= _____

c. Using your answer to part *b*, determine the area (in square feet) of a circular garden enclosed with a 60-foot fence. Round your answer to the nearest square foot.

d. Use the keystrokes from part *b* and your calculator tool to fill in the chart below. The chart compares the area of a square garden plot to that of a circular garden plot enclosed by a fence of a given length.   The lengths of the sides of a square garden are all the same and are equal to 1/4 of the total amount of fencing. Round your computations for area to the nearest square foot.

Amount of Fencing in Feet	Side of Square Garden in Feet (1/4 • amount of fencing)	Area of Square in Square Feet (side • side)	Area of Circle in Square Feet
50			$\dfrac{50^2}{4\pi} =$
70			$\dfrac{70^2}{4\pi} =$
85			$\dfrac{85^2}{4\pi} =$
92			$\dfrac{92^2}{4\pi} =$
112			$\dfrac{112^2}{4\pi}$

e. In general, for a given length of fence, does it appear that a square garden plot or a circular garden plot would give you more space? Justify your answer with data. What other considerations might affect the shape you choose for your garden?

_____

_____

_____

_____

_____

4. Extension Exercise—A Recipe for Soil Replacement

Sometimes when a garden is planted in a spot for the first time, the soil may need preparation beyond fertilization. This is particularly true in geographic locations with sandy, rocky, or hard clay soil. In such cases, you might dig up the existing soil and replace it with more fertile soil. Depending on the quality of the existing soil, you might need to dig 6 to 12 inches deep.

a. Using the following recipe for soil replacement, determine how many cubic feet of soil would be created from one batch of the recipe. To do this, convert each ingredient in the recipe to cubic feet. Round to the nearest 1/2 (0.5) cubic foot.

(1 gallon = 0.1337 cubic foot, 4 quarts = 1 gallon)

Fertile Soil Replacement Recipe

1 bale of peat moss   6 cubic feet

22 gallons of sand   (*Hint:* 22 gal × 0.1337 = the amount in cubic feet.)

_____ cubic feet

30 gallons of coarse vermiculite (about 1 large bag)   _____ cubic feet

6 gallons of wood ashes and charcoal   _____ cubic feet

26 gallons of compost   _____ cubic feet

1 quart of lime (*Hint:* 1/4 gal × 0.1337 = the amount in cubic feet.)

_____ cubic feet

1 quart of fertilizer   _____ cubic feet

Total cubic feet   _____ cubic feet

When the above quantities are mixed together, the "whole does not equal the sum of the parts." This happens because some of the smaller particles, such as the sand, move into the empty spaces of the more porous ingredients. Once the ingredients are mixed, the recipe creates about 16 cubic feet of fertile soil.

b. In the table below, determine how many cubic feet of soil would be replaced in each garden plot for the different depths. To compute the number of cubic feet, multiply the length times the width times the depth (in feet).

Garden Plot Size	Cubic Feet Replaced If Soil is Dug:		
	½ Foot (or 6 in.) Deep	¾ Foot (or 9 in.) Deep	1 Foot (or 12 in.) Deep
8 ft by 12 ft			
4 ft by 4 ft			
4 garden plots, each 4 ft by 4 ft			

c. How many batches of the recipe would have to be made for each of the gardens below? Show how you determined the number of batches.

4 ft by 4 ft, 6 inches deep.   Number of batches: _____

4 ft by 4 ft, 9 inches deep.   Number of batches: _____

8 ft by 12 ft, 12 inches deep.   Number of batches: _____

Chapter 2—Equations, Inequalities, and Problem Solving
Key Concept Activity #2: A Chill in the Air

1.   Extension Exercise—How Hot Is It?

2.   Conceptual Exercise—Comparing Temperatures

3.   Group Activity—Zoya's Investments

4.   Open Environment Activity—Fruit Salad

1. Extension Exercise—How Hot Is It?

In the United States, temperature is generally reported in degrees Fahrenheit. Most of the world, however, measures temperature in degrees Celsius. During the Olympics, for example, the temperatures are reported in degrees Celsius. We may have to convert from degrees Celsius to degrees Fahrenheit (or the reverse) in order to appreciate how hot or cold it is outside.

Formula for converting from degrees <u>Celsius *C* to Fahrenheit *F*</u>: $F = 32 + \dfrac{9}{5} C$

a. Solve the formula $F = 32 + \dfrac{9}{5} C$ for *C* to obtain a formula for converting from degrees Fahrenheit (F) to degrees Celsius (C).

b. Fill in the chart below by converting between degrees Celsius and degrees Fahrenheit. Round your answers to the nearest tenth of a degree.

Celsius Temperature	Fahrenheit Temperature
-15°	
9°	
32°	
63°	
115°	
	-31°
	0°
	15°
	50°
	100°
	212°

The lowest temperatures (in degrees Fahrenheit) recorded in the United States are shown in the graph below. They occurred in Alaska, Colorado, Idaho, Minnesota, Montana, North Dakota, Utah, and Wyoming.

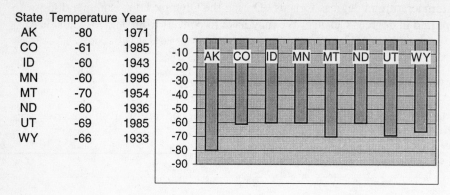

State	Temperature	Year
AK	-80	1971
CO	-61	1985
ID	-60	1943
MN	-60	1996
MT	-70	1954
ND	-60	1936
UT	-69	1985
WY	-66	1933

Answer the following questions based on the graph and table above.

c. Let x represent the recorded low temperature. Write a compound inequality representing the range of temperatures that x lies between.

d. Graph the compound inequality from part *c*.

-120° -100° -80°   -60   -40°   -20°   0°   20°

e. What was the lowest recorded temperature ever in the United States?

f. In what year and state was the lowest recorded temperature?

2. Conceptual Exercise—Comparing Temperatures

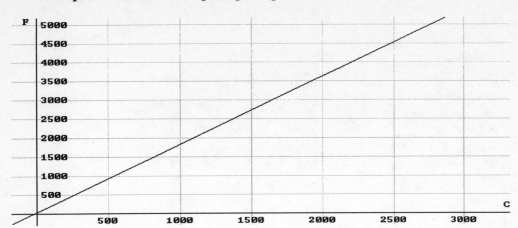

a. Use the graph to estimate the equivalent Fahrenheit temperatures for the given Celsius temperatures and vice versa. Mark the point on the graph relating to each conversion.

- Freezing temperature of water: 32° F = _____° C

- Boiling temperature of water: 100° C = _____° F

- Temperature at which equal amounts of salt and water freeze: 0° F = _____° C

- Absolute zero (minimum of molecular movement): -273° C = _____° F

- Melting point of gold: 1063 ° C = _____° F

- Boiling point of gold: 2660° C = _____° F

b. Convert each of the temperatures given above with the formula F = 32 + 9/5 C. Show your substitutions and solve the equation when necessary. Round answers to the nearest degree.

- Freezing temperature of water: 32° F = _____° C

- Boiling temperature of water: 100° C = _____° F

- Temperature at which equal amounts of salt and water freeze: 0° F = _____° C

- Absolute zero (minimum of molecular movement): -273° C = _____° F

- Melting point of gold: 1063 ° C = _____° F

- Boiling point of gold: 2660° C = _____° F

The following chart shows temperatures (in °F) for selected towns in Oregon on May 17, 1998.

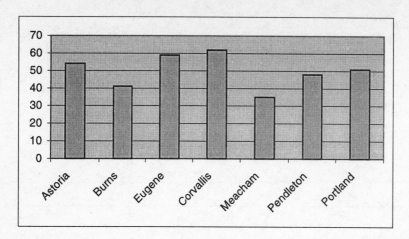

c. Solve the equation $F = 32 + \dfrac{9}{5}C$ for C (or copy the answer from the Extension Exercise).

d. What is the approximate range of temperatures (in °F) for towns in Oregon on May 17, 1998? Using the variable F, write a compound inequality that describes that range of temperatures.

e. In the compound inequality in part *d*, replace the variable F with the equivalent expression containing C. Solve the resulting inequality to find the range of temperatures expressed in degrees Celsius.

3. Group Activity—Zoya's Investments

Zoya just received a $25,000 advance and needs to make at least $1425 annual interest from investing this money. She has decided to place the money in two accounts--a relatively safe account paying 5% simple interest and a high risk account paying 7% simple interest. To help her decide how much money should be placed in the accounts, follow the steps below.

Step 1: UNDERSTAND the Problem.

a. Fill in the following table to see how much interest Zoya would earn from dividing the $25,000 between the two accounts in various ways.

Amount Invested at 5%	Amount Invested at 7% (Rest of $25,000)	Annual Interest from 5% Account $I = PRT$	Annual Interest from 7% Account $I = PRT$	Total Annual Interest from Both Accounts
$0	$25,000	$I = 0(0.05)(1)$ $= \$0$	$I = 25000(0.05)(1)$ $= \$1750$	$0 + 1750 =$ $\$1750$
$5,000				
$10,000				
$15,000				
$20,000				
$25,000				

Step 2: ASSIGN a variable to an unknown in the problem.

b. List all of the unknowns. Let $x =$ the amount invested at 5%. Use the table from part *a* to help you write an expression in x to represent the amount invested in the 7% account.

Step 3: ILLUSTRATE the problem.

c. Fill in the chart. Put the information given and the variable expressions in the appropriate boxes. Use the formula to determine the variable expression for the interest earned.

	Principal	•	Rate	•	Time	=	Interest
5% Account							
7% Account							
Total			**********				

Step 4: TRANSLATE the problem into a mathematical model.

d. Write an equation in x to aid in solving the word problem.

Step 5: COMPLETE the work by solving the equation.

e. Solve the equation in part *d* for x.

Step 6: INTERPRET the results.

f. Check the solution and summarize the result in words. What would you suggest Zoya do?

_____

_____

_____

_____

4. Open Environment Activity—Fruit Salad

You've started a catering business and have been asked to quote a price per person for catering fruit salad at an afternoon reception for 20 people. The recipe you will use is given below.

<u>Fruit Salad</u>
2   pounds green grapes, halved
3   pounds watermelon, cubed
1   pint fresh blueberries
$1\frac{1}{4}$ pounds nectarines or mangos, sliced
1 6-ounce can frozen pineapple juice concentrate
Combine ingredients and serve chilled. Serves 10 guests.

The wholesale prices for the ingredients are as shown below.

green grapes	84 cents a pound
watermelon	21 cents a pound
blueberries	92 cents a pint
mangos	50 cents a pound
pineapple juice concentrate	43 cents a can

a. Enter the name, quantity, and unit price of each ingredient into a spreadsheet to compute the cost of each item and the total cost for all of the ingredients. Record your results below.

Ingredient	Quantity	Unit Price	Total Price
Green grapes			
Watermelon			
Blueberries			
Mangos			
Pineapple juice concentrate			
			Total Cost:

b. *Cost per serving* is the amount you pay, per person, for your raw materials. Using the information from the spreadsheet, write an equation that relates the cost per serving, *C*, to the total cost for all of the ingredients. (Remember that the salad will serve 20 people.)

c. Estimate the time it will take you to buy the ingredients and to make the fruit salad once you have them. Record your estimates in hours.

Estimated time for trip to grocery store (roundtrip plus shopping time): _____

Estimated time to make the fruit salad: _____

d. The salad must be delivered, and you estimate it will take about an hour to deliver the salad and set up the table. Later you will return to pick up the salad bowl and clean the table, which you estimate will take about a half-hour. Compute the total time you estimate it will take to buy ingredients, make the salad, deliver the salad, and pick up the salad bowl.

Total time spent: _____

e. Since you are trying to make catering your sole business, you determine that you need to make about $20 an hour for your time on each catering event. Use the result of part *d* to determine how much you would have to earn in profit (over the cost of the salad) to make $20 an hour for your time.

f. Letting *p* be price per serving, set up an equation and solve it to determine how much you should charge per person for the salad. (First determine the total price as total cost of salad + profit. Divide the total price among the 20 servings.)

Chapter 3—Graphing
Key Concept Activity #3: The Race

1. Conceptual Exercise—Depreciating the Company Car

2. Open Environment Activity—Income and Tax Liability

3. Group Activity—Analyzing the Federal Income Tax System

4. Extension Exercise—Racing with Michael

1. Conceptual Exercise—Depreciating the Company Car

Suppose the Mountain Bike Shop buys a company car for $18,000 and decides to depreciate it over a six-year period using straight-line depreciation. This means that the value of the car will decrease by $3000 each year. The constant rate of change implies that the value of the car will depreciate linearly.

a. Complete the following table that shows the value of the car over time.

Time t (years)	Value V (thousands of dollars)
0	18
1	15
2	
3	
4	
5	
6	

b. Plot all of the data points on the coordinate plane below and connect them to form a line.

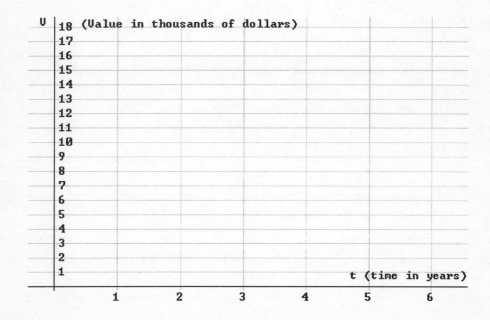

c. Select any two ordered pairs of the form (t, V) from part b and find the slope of the line using the formula:

$$\text{Slope} = \frac{\text{Vertical Change}}{\text{Horizontal Change}}$$

Slope =

d. State the ordered pair that represents the vertical intercept point (y-intercept point).

Vertical intercept point: (_____ , _____)

e. State the ordered pair that represents the horizontal intercept point (x-intercept point).

Horizontal intercept point: (_____ , _____)

f. Explain what your slope and intercepts mean in terms of the depreciation of the car.

_____

_____

_____

_____

_____

_____

2.   Open Environment Activity—Income and Tax Liability

Consider the 1997 federal tax rate schedule for people whose filing status is single. Note: Any reference to *income* means *taxable income*.

If your income is		Your tax liability (tax owed) is	Of any income over-
Over-	But not over-		
$0	$24,650	-------------- 15%	$0
24,650	59,750	$3,697.50 + 28%	24,650
59,750	124,650	13,525.50 + 31%	59,750
124,650	271,050	33,644.50 + 36%	124,650
271,050	---------	86,348.50 + 39.6%	271,050

Your goal is to develop a set of equations that will tell us how much federal tax must be paid at different income levels. Suppose x represents a person's income and y is the tax liability (tax that must be paid to the federal government on that income). The equations you will construct should express tax liability as a function of income.

a.   The first row of numbers in the tax rate schedule mean that if your income is $0 - $24,650, then your tax liability is 15% of your income. Use the tools in the Open Environment to help fill in the table below, which calculates the tax liability for a range of incomes within this first bracket.

Income, x	Tax Liability, y
$0	
4,000	
8,000	
12,000	
16,000	
20,000	
24,000	

b.   Explain the pattern in the table by completing the following sentence.

As the income increases by $4000, the tax liability _____

_____

c.   Select two ordered pairs, (x, y), from the data table and use them to calculate the slope. Express your slope as a decimal.

d. Explain the connection between the slope and the tax rate.

_____

_____

_____

_____

e. Plot all of the data points in the table. Connect the data points to form a straight line.

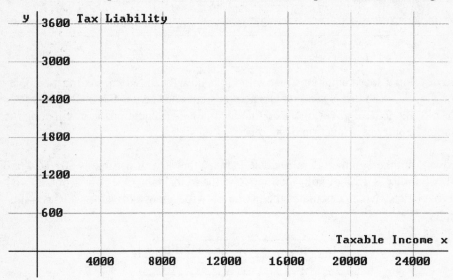

f. What is the vertical intercept point or *y*-intercept point? (____ , ____)

g. A linear equation in two variables can be written in the form $y = mx + b$, where *m* is the slope and *b* is the *y*-intercept. What is the equation that represents tax liability *y* in terms of income *x* for the 15% tax bracket?

_____

h. In the Open Environment, graph the formula you obtained in part *g*. Then explain how the graph can verify if your formula correctly fits the data.

_____

_____

_____

3. Group Activity—Analyzing the Federal Income Tax System

Refer to the tax table and situation in the Open Environment Activity—Income and Tax Liability (p. 19 of this workbook) to complete the questions below. The second row of numbers from the table can be translated as follows: If your income is over $24,650 but not over $59,750, your tax liability is $3,697.50 plus 28% of any income over $24,650.

a. Work with your group members to fill in the table below, which calculates the tax liability for several incomes within this second bracket.

Income, x	Tax Calculation	Tax Liability, y
$28,000		$4635.50
32,000		
36,000		
40,000		
44,000		
48,000		
52,000		
56,000		

b. If x is the income, then write an expression for calculating "28% of income over $24,650" in terms of x?

_____

c. Work with your group members and use the information from part *b* to find the linear equation that represents tax liability y in terms of income x for the 28% tax bracket. Simplify your equation so that it is in the form $y = mx + b$.

d. Each group member needs to choose two ordered pairs, (x, y), from the data table and use them to calculate the slope. Try to have each group member select a different set of ordered pairs and compare results with the group.

Slope calculations:

e. What is the connection between your group's slope calculations in part *d* and the coefficient m found in part *c*? What does the slope mean in terms of the problem situation?

_____

_____

_____

f. Your group is given the task of finding equations (formulas) for each of the three remaining tax brackets. Discuss as a group the best way to accomplish this task.

31% Bracket: _____

36% Bracket: _____

39.6% Bracket: _____

g. Substitute each income listed below into the appropriate formula from part *f*. Then calculate the tax liability for a single person with that income.

- $100,000

- $200,000

- $300,000

h. How does the U.S. tax system affect different incomes? Explain the advantages (if any) and disadvantages (if any) of moving up to a higher income tax bracket.

_____

_____

_____

_____

_____

_____

4. Extension Exercise—Racing with Michael

In Key Concept Activity #3: The Race, we compared the slopes and y-intercepts of two linear equations that expressed distance (in meters) as a function of time (in seconds), i.e.,

$$\text{Michael's equation}: d = 10t$$
$$\text{Your equation}: d = 7t + 100$$

Use these two equations to help you with this exercise.

a. You won the 200-meter race in just under 15 seconds. Set up and solve an equation that will give the exact winning time.

b. Using the winning time from part *a*, find out how far ahead of Michael you were when you crossed the finish line.

c. In the 400-meter race, Michael caught up with you and moved on to win the race. Set up and solve an equation that will give the exact time when Michael ran past you on his way to the finish line.

d. Assuming that Michael and you keep running at the same speed, explain why Michael must eventually catch you, no matter how much of a head start you receive. What part of the linear equation immediately tells you this fact?

_____

_____

_____

e. Michael's paradox:

The race starts with a 100-meter gap (interval) between Michael and you. In the amount of time it takes Michael to reach the 100-meter mark, you will have run to a new point further on. So Michael has a new gap to close. But, in the time it takes Michael to reach this new point, you will have run to another new point further on. So Michael has another new gap to close. Michael knows the gaps keep getting smaller, but there will always be one more gap to close (an infinite number). If this process continues, how can Michael ever close the gap completely?

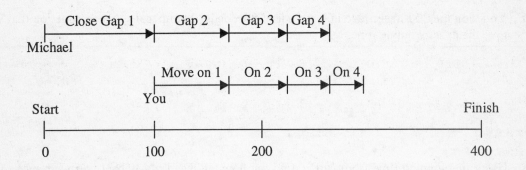

Explain the fallacy in the above argument. *Hint:* What assumptions are made about time?

_____

_____

_____

_____

_____

_____

_____

_____

Chapter 4—Exponents and Polynomials
Key Concept Activity #4: Information Skyway

1. Extension Exercise—Earth to Earth

2. Conceptual Exercise—Looking Back in Time

3. Open Environment Activity—Computing Distances

4. Group Activity—Accidental Deaths

1.   Extension Exercise—Earth to Earth

A satellite that is 22,245 miles from the earth's surface travels at the same rotational speed as the earth in order to stay in orbit. At this distance from Earth, the satellite is visible from an area covering 1/3 of the surface of the earth and is no more than 24,470 miles from an observer anywhere in this area. For a live satellite broadcast to travel from China to the United States, its signal (which travels at the speed of light) must zigzag from a transmitter in China to one satellite, from that satellite to another receiver/transmitter on Earth, then on to a second satellite, and finally back to another receiver/transmitter in the United States.

You will need a calculator and the information below as you work through this exercise. To use the circumference formula and distance formula correctly, the units have to match. For example, in the distance formula, if the rate is given in miles per hour, then distance must be measured in miles and the time in hours.

Radius of Earth:	3960 miles
Speed of light:	186,000 or 1.86×10^5 miles per second
	982,080,000 or 9.8208×10^8 feet per second
	669,600,000 or 6.696×10^8 miles per hour
	1,080,000,000 or 1.08×10^9 kilometers per hour
Circumference Formula:	$C = 2\pi r$, where C is the circumference and r is the radius
Distance Formula:	$d = rt$, where d is distance, r is speed (or rate), and t is time

a.   Assume the average distance from an earth location to a satellite is 23,500 miles. Traveling through two satellites as described above, how long does it take a news anchorperson in the United States to receive a signal broadcast live from a correspondent in China? Give your answer to the nearest hundredth of a second. Show how you arrived at your answer and draw a diagram showing the path and distances that the signal might travel. *Hint:* You do not need to know the distance between the United States and China to solve this problem.

b.   Compare the speed of satellite communication in part *a* to talking on telephone lines where signals are sent around the surface of the earth in a more direct path either as electrons through a wire or as light signals through fiber optic cables. Find how long a signal takes from the United States to China by way of telephone wires. To approximate the distance that the signal may travel, compute the circumference of the earth and approximate the distance from the United States to China as halfway around the world. *Hint:* Assume that electrons travel at the speed of light, and round your result to the nearest hundredth of a second.

A signal sent over the Internet will find an available route, but not necessarily the shortest path, to reach its destination. For example, a message from Cincinnati to Boston may go from Cincinnati to Los Angeles, to New York, to Dallas, to Sydney Australia, to England, and finally to Boston. Along the way, there are many switching stations that may delay a signal.

c. Assuming no time was lost at switching stations, determine how many miles an e-mail message (traveling at the speed of light) has traveled if it takes 10 minutes to go from Casper, Wyoming to Missoula, Montana. *Hint:* Use the fact that there are 60 seconds in a minute to solve this problem.

d. Write a brief explanation of why a telephone conversation between cities that are 5000 miles apart appears to be in "real time" with no apparent delay between what is said and what is heard. Then, explain why there may be a noticeable lag in satellite broadcasts from across the seas or a delay of several minutes in receiving a message over the Internet.

_____

_____

_____

_____

_____

_____

_____

_____

2. Conceptual Exercise—Looking Back in Time

Astronomers say that when we see the stars, we are looking back in time because we see something as it looked in the past. When we see a star "burn out," it may have died years ago, but it has taken that long for the light of the explosion to reach Earth. Use a calculator in this exercise.

a. Find out how far light travels in the given length of time? Write your answers in scientific notation. Use formulas from Extension Exercise—Earth to Earth on page 33.

   24 hours? ____
   one week? ____
   one year? ____

b. If we see a star burn out and an astronomer has determined that the star burned out about 10 years earlier, how far was the star from Earth? Write your answer in scientific notation and include correct units with your answer.

c. A "light year" is the distance that light travels in one year. To answer the following questions, determine how many hours are in a year and then use the speed of light information in the first exercise. There are 365 days in a year. Write your answers in scientific notation.

   Measured in kilometers, how long is a light year? _____

   Measured in miles, how long is a light year? _____

d. If a star is 30 light years away, how many miles is the star from Earth? Write your answer in scientific notation and include correct units.

e. If you could travel at the speed of light, how long would it take you to travel to a star that is 30 light years away?

f. Fill in the blanks of the chart below. Write the distances in scientific notation and record the time it would take a signal (traveling at the speed of light) to travel from the sun to each planet.

Planet	Distance from Sun (in km)	Distance (scientific notation)	Time to Receive Message from Sun
Mercury	57,910,000		
Venus	108,200,000		
Earth	149,600,000		
Mars	227,940,000		
Jupiter	778,330,000		
Saturn	1,429,400,000		
Uranus	2,870,990,000		
Neptune	4,504,000,000		
Pluto	5,913,520,000		

3. Open Environment Activity—Computing Distances

When a rock is dropped from the edge of a cliff that is 400 feet above the ground, the approximate distance (in feet) of the rock from the ground after t seconds can be computed by the formula,

$$d = (-4t + 20)(4t + 20).$$

a. Multiply the binomial factors in the previous formula to obtain a different form of this equation.

$$d = \underline{\hspace{5cm}}$$

b. Use the graphing tool to graph $d = (-4t + 20)(4t + 20)$. Then graph the rewritten formula for d that you obtained in part *a.* If your two graphs are not identical, check your multiplication. Show your graph below for the first 5 seconds after the rock is dropped.

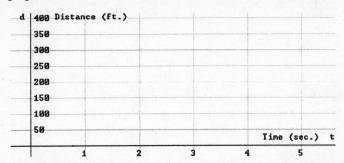

c. Find the formula for the distance (in feet) that the rock falls after t seconds. (*Hint:* the formula you have gives the distance of the rock from the *bottom of the cliff.* The distance of the rock falling is measured from the *top of the cliff.*)

$$d = \underline{\hspace{5cm}} \cdot 16t^2$$

d. How far has the rock fallen in 5 seconds? Show or explain how you came up with your answer.

e. How far is the rock from the ground after falling for 5 seconds? Show or explain how you came up with your answer.

f. Use the spreadsheet tool to fill in the missing data in the chart. Calculate and record in the middle column for how far the rock has fallen at various points in time. To get a better understanding of the speed of light, compute how far a light signal would travel in the same length of time. (To calculate the distance light travels, use $d = rt$.)

Time (in sec)	Distance Rock Falls (in ft)	Distance Light Travels (in mi)
0	0	
1	16	
2	64	
3		
4		
5		

Notice from the table that the Earth's gravitational pull causes the rock to speed up as it falls, so in the last second it falls further than in the first second. A light signal travels at a constant speed and therefore travels the same distance during each second.

4. Group Activity—Accidental Deaths

Record the time when you start this exercise. Start time: _____.

According to data from the National Safety Council, a polynomial that represents the annual number of deaths due to motor vehicle accidents over the period of 1990 - 1994 is
$$46,426 - 4381x + 893x^2$$ where $x = 0, 1,..., 4$ represents the years 1990, 1991,..., 1994.

Also based on data from the National Safety Council, a polynomial representing the annual number of deaths due to all other types of accidents over the period of 1990 - 1994 is
$$33,139 - 2540x + 730x^2$$ where $x = 0, 1, ..., 4$ represents the years 1990, 1991,..., 1994.

a. Use the polynomials to complete the table below. Find the number of accidental deaths per year over the period of 1990 - 1994 by evaluating each polynomial at the given values of x.

Year	x	Number of Accidental Deaths Due to Motor Vehicle Accidents	Number of Accidental Deaths Due to All Other Types of Accidents	Total Number of Accidental Deaths
1990	0			
1991	1			
1992	2			
1993	3			
1994	4			

b. Use the given polynomials above to find a polynomial that represents the total number of accidental deaths per year. Evaluate this polynomial for $x = 0, 1, 2, 3, 4$ and compare your answers to the last column in part *a*. Show your substitutions and answers in the chart below.

Polynomial, P = _____

x	Value of x substituted into P	P evaluated at x-value	Data from last column in part *a*
0			
1			
2			
3			
4			

c. Create a bar graph that represents the data for total accidental deaths and for number of accidental deaths due to motor vehicles for the years 1990 - 1994. Use one color to represent total accidental deaths and another color to represent accidental deaths due to motor vehicles. Be sure to label your axes and create an appropriate scale.

d. Look at the graph you created in part c. During what year was the difference between total accidental deaths and accidental deaths due to motor vehicles the smallest?

e. When your group is finished with this activity, record the ending time.
Ending time: _____

f. How far could a signal traveling at the speed of light have traveled during the time it took your group to work through the activity?

Chapter 5—Factoring Polynomials
Key Concept Activity #5: More Space for Bruin

1.   Extension Exercise—Out the Back Door, Bruin

2.   Conceptual Exercise—Don't Get Egg on Your Face

3.   Open Environment Activity—More Space, Less Bruin

4.   Group Activity—The 10-Meter Dive

1. Extension Exercise—Out the Back Door, Bruin

In Key Concept Activity #5: More Space for Bruin, you have 200 feet of fencing available and need to build a rectangular pen. Your goal was to find the dimensions that would give the family dog, Bruin, the maximum area to live in. Suppose you decide to build a rectangular pen along the back of the house so that you only need to fence in three sides (i.e., the house is the fourth side and would not need fencing).

a. Draw a sketch of the rectangular pen in its location against the back of the house. Label the side opposite the house as x and the two sides connecting the x-side to the house as y.

b. Write an equation for the fencing needed using only variables x and y and the 200 feet of fencing that will enclose the three sides of the pen.

c. Isolate x in the equation from part *b*. Your equation for x should be written in terms of y.

d. The area of a rectangle is length times width, and so we have the formula $A = x \bullet y$ to figure out how to give Bruin the maximum play space. Substitute the expression you obtained for x from part *c* into the area formula so that A is written only in terms of the variable y.

e. Find the two sets of dimensions that can be used to build a rectangular pen with an area of 4800 square feet by substituting 4800 for A in the equation from part *d*. Solve this quadratic equation by factoring to find y. Then substitute into the expression for x in part *c*. *Hint:* First put the quadratic equation in standard form, i.e., $ax^2 + bx + c = 0$.

f. Explain how two sets of dimensions can give Bruin the same area to play in.

_____

_____

_____

g. Fill in the following table to observe whether you can find an area for the pen using dimensions that will give you more space than 4800 square feet. Remember that you have 200 feet of fencing. Use your expression for x in part c and the area formula $A = (\text{length } y) \bullet (\text{width } x)$ to complete the table.

Length y (feet)	Width x (feet)	Area A (sq. ft)
10		
20		
30		
40		
50		
60		
70		
80		
90		

h. Based on the table above, what dimensions will produce the maximum area for Bruin?

_____

i. There are other possible dimensions we could use that are not listed in the table, such as 45 ft by 110 ft, or 55 ft by 90 ft. If you think that the dimensions from part g give the maximum area, explain why; otherwise, find any dimensions that will produce more space for Bruin.

_____

_____

_____

_____

2. Conceptual Exercise—Don't Get Egg on Your Face

Suppose you throw an egg vertically into the air from a height of 6 feet above the ground at an initial velocity of 46 feet per second. The equation of motion for a free falling body tells you that the height h in feet of the egg in t seconds can be modeled by the quadratic equation

$$h = -16t^2 + 46t + 6.$$

a. To find when the egg strikes the ground, let height $h = 0$ and solve the resulting equation by factoring.

b. Which of the solutions to part *a* makes sense in terms of the problem situation? Remember that t represents time in seconds. Use complete sentences to explain your answer.

_____

_____

_____

_____

_____

_____

_____

c. Sketch a graph of distance *h* as a function of time *t* on the coordinate plane below. Estimate the point on the curve where the egg reaches its maximum height.

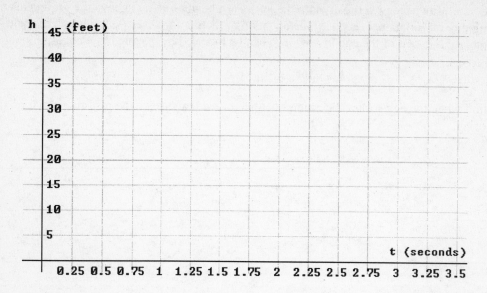

d. What is your estimate for the maximum height and when did the egg reach that height? Use a complete sentence to express your answer.

_____

_____

_____

e. If velocity is the change in distance with respect to time, explain when you think the egg is traveling at its fastest and slowest speed.

_____

_____

_____

_____

_____

3. Open Environment Activity—More Space, Less Bruin

Suppose you want to plant a rectangular-shaped vegetable garden, but you need to protect it from your neighbor's crazy dog, Bruin. Although Bruin is kept in a pen, his owners often forget to latch the gate securely. You have not seen the dog escape yet but plan to use 18 meters of wire fencing to enclose the perimeter of your garden, just in case. Assuming that you use all 18 meters, what dimensions will give you the maximum amount of area for planting?

a. Draw a picture of your garden labeling the length x and the width y.

b. Substitute the 18 meters of wiring for Perimeter in the equation below and then isolate one of the variables so that your resulting equation is in terms of one variable only.

$$\text{Perimeter} = 2(x + y)$$

c. Substitute the expression for the variable that you isolated in part *b* into the area equation below.

$$A = x \bullet y$$

d. Find the dimensions that are needed to build a rectangular garden with an area of 8 square meters, by substituting 8 for A in the equation obtained in part *c*. Solve this quadratic equation by factoring. *Hint:* First put the equation in standard form, i.e., $ax^2 + bx + c = 0$.

e. Repeat part *d* for gardens with the following areas:
- 14 square meters
- 18 square meters
- 20 square meters

f. Can you build a garden with an area greater than 20 square meters? Use the tools in the Open Environment to complete the following table.

Length (meters)	Width (meters)	Perimeter (meters)	Area (sq. m)
4.1			
4.2			
4.3			
4.4			
4.5			
4.6			
4.7			
4.8			
4.9			

g. Using the tools in the Open Environment, graph the quadratic equation from part *c.*

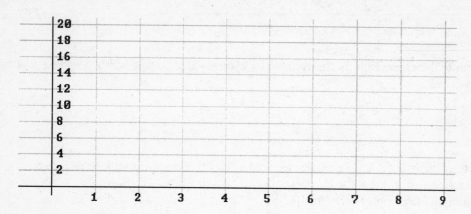

h. What dimensions give the maximum area for planting a garden? _____

i. Based on the calculations you have made for Bruin's play area, what special type of rectangular shape will produce maximum area with a fixed perimeter?

4. Group Activity—The 10-Meter Dive

Suppose a diver jumps from a platform that is 10 meters above the surface of the water at an initial velocity of 5 meters per second. The height, h (in meters), of the diver's position above the water at any time t (in seconds) is given by the following equation:

$$h = -5t^2 + 5t + 10.$$

a. How many seconds, after jumping, does it take the diver to enter the water? To answer this question, let $h = 0$ and solve by factoring.

b. Complete the table to see how the height of the diver's position changes from 0 to 2½ seconds. Round to the nearest hundredth of a meter, if necessary.

Time, t (seconds)	Height, h (meters)
0	
.25	
.50	
.75	
1.00	
1.25	
1.50	
1.75	
2.00	
2.25	
2.50	

c. Explain how the height of the diver's position changed over the interval of time in the table.

_____

_____

_____

_____

_____

d. How many seconds after the jump did the diver reach a maximum height? What is that maximum height? Write your answer in a complete sentence.

_____

_____

_____

e. Sketch a graph of the height equation over the time interval given in the table for part *b*. What part of the curve makes no sense in terms of the problem situation? Explain your reasoning.

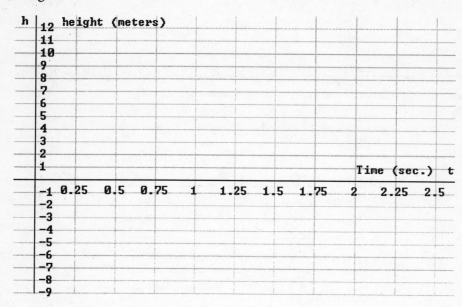

_____

_____

_____

_____

Chapter 6—Rational Expressions
Key Concept Activity #6: Affording a Car

1.   Extension Exercise—Financing Jamille's Car

2.   Conceptual Exercise—Floor Plan

3.   Group Activity—Go the Distance

4.   Open Environment Activity—Children's Doses of Medicine

1. **Extension Exercise—Financing Jamille's Car**

Jamille has found the car of his dreams and has negotiated a price of $15,798 after trading in his old car. He will use his trade-in as a down payment. Here are his options for a 4-year loan:

*   Option 1: $1000 rebate with an 8.9% loan
*   Option 2: 7.7% loan with no rebate
*   Option 3: 9.1% home equity loan

To determine the monthly payment, the formula is: $L \cdot \dfrac{r(1+r)^n}{(1+r)^n - 1}$ where L is the amount financed, r is the monthly interest rate (annual rate $\div$ 12) and n is the number of months of the loan.

> *Calculator keystrokes for computing the monthly payment by the formula above:*
>   *Example*: To compute a monthly payment for a $12,000, 3-year loan at 8.5% annual rate.
> * $L = 12,000$
> * $n = 36$ (3 years at 12 months per year)
> * $r = 0.0071$ (that is 0.085/12 rounded to the nearest ten-thousandth)
> * $1 + r = 1.0071$ (that is $1 + 0.0071$)
> Monthly payment = $\boxed{12000}\;\boxed{(}\;\boxed{(}\;\boxed{0.0071}\;\boxed{\times}\;\boxed{1.0071}\;\boxed{y^x}\;\boxed{36}\;\boxed{)}\;\boxed{\div}\;\boxed{(}\;\boxed{(}\;\boxed{1.0071}\;\boxed{y^x}\;\boxed{36}\;\boxed{-}\;\boxed{1}\;\boxed{)}$

If Jamille chooses the plan with the rebate, then he will apply the rebate to his down payment and finance the remaining amount.

a. Find the monthly payment for each of Jamille's three options using the monthly payment formula above. In the third column of the chart below, show how the values for n, L, and r are substituted into the formula. Round r to the nearest thousandth. In the fourth column, record the monthly payment to the nearest cent. (Remember that this is a 4-year loan.)

Financing Option	Amount Financed	Values Substituted into Formula	Monthly Payment
1. $1000 rebate with a rate of 8.9%	$L = \$14,798$		
2. 7.7% loan with no rebate	$L = \$15,798$		
3. 9.1% home equity loan	$L = \$15,798$		

b. For each payment option, write the total amount of the payments, *A*, paid on each loan after the 48 monthly payments.

Option 1, $1000 rebate, 8.9% rate: _A =_ _____

Option 2, No rebate, 7.7% rate: _A =_ _____

Option 3, No rebate, 9.1% rate: _A =_ _____

c. The total interest paid is the total of the payments minus the original loan amount. Fill in the following table to compare Jamille's cost of buying the car using the different financing options. If necessary, round amounts to the nearest cent.

	$1000 Rebate 8.9% Rate	No Rebate 7.7% Rate	Home Equity Loan 9.1% Rate
Amount Financed (From chart on previous page)			
Total Payments (Use formulas from part *b.*)			
Total Interest Paid (Total Payments - Amount Financed)			
Money Saved in Taxes on Home Equity Loan	$0	$0	(28% of the total interest from the above line)
Cost after Tax Savings (Total Payments Minus Tax Savings)			

d. Based on the data from part *c*, explain to Jamille which option would be the best after all of the information has been considered. Include the data to support your conclusions.

_____

_____

_____

_____

2. Conceptual Exercise—Floor Plan

Below is a drawing to scale of space occupied by three businesses in a building.

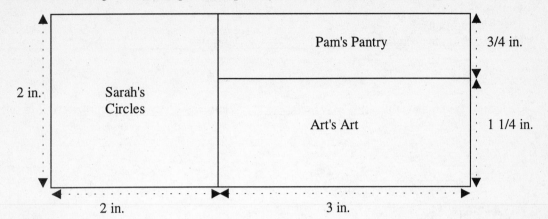

a. On the drawing, what are the dimensions (in inches) of each company?

Sarah's Circles _____   Pam's Pantry _____

Art's Art _____

b. Pam has measured the width (the shorter dimension) of her company and found it to be 30 feet wide. Set up and solve a proportion to determine how long her space is (in feet).

Proportion: _____   Length = _____ feet

The heating bill for the building is sent to the landlord who then divides the bill among the three businesses so that each company's share is proportional to the amount of floor space it occupies in the building. Sarah is curious how much the other businesses are paying for heat. She decides to determine the area of the floor space of each company and set up a proportion to determine the amount charged to each company.

c. Set up and solve proportions to determine the length and width (in feet) of all three
    companies' spaces. Compute the area (square feet) of each of the three spaces. *Hint:*
    You will need to use the information from part *b* about Pam's space to solve this problem.

Sarah's company:
    Proportion for length: _____ Length = _____

    Proportion for width: _____ Width = _____

    Area = _____

Art's company:
    Proportion for length: _____ Length = _____

    Proportion for width: _____ Width = _____

    Area = _____

Pam's company:
    Length = _____   Width = _____   Area = _____

d. Sarah was charged $750 for her share of the heating bill. If the bill was shared correctly
    according to the floor space occupied by each company, determine Pam's and Art's shares of
    the heating bills. *Hint:* For Art's share, for example, set up a proportion in which the ratio of
    Sarah's share of the heating bill to her amount (area) of floor space is equal to the related
    ratio for Art's business. Solve the proportion for the unknown (Art's share). Set up and solve
    a similar proportion for Pam's share.

Art's company:
Proportion: _____   Share of heating bill: _____

Pam's company:
Proportion: _____   Share of heating bill: _____

3. Group Activity—Go the Distance

a. Pick a path in a room or hallway (from front to back, for example) that is easy to measure and to walk. Measure this path in meters.

Length of path: _____ meters

b. Have three group members travel the path, one at a time, as described below, while the other group members watch and record the time it took (in seconds). To clock the time, use a stop watch or a digital watch that displays seconds.

Group Member 1: Walk at a normal pace. Time = _____ seconds.

Group Member 2: Walk fast with long strides. Time = _____ seconds.

Group Member 3: Walk very slowly. Time = _____ seconds.

The distance traveled at a speed (or rate r) in time t is given by the formula, $d = rt$. For this formula to be valid, the units used throughout have to match. For example, if time is given in hours and speed is given in miles per hour, then the distance is measured in miles. If distance is measured in feet and time is measured in minutes, then the speed is measured in feet per minute.

c. Solve the distance formula for the variable r so that r is represented by a rational expression.

d. Use the rational expression from part c to compute the speed at which each group member walked the path. Use your calculator and round to the nearest tenth. Include correct units with your answers.

Group member 1: $r = $ _____

Group member 2: $r = $ _____

Group member 3: $r = $ _____

3. **Group Activity—Go the Distance** Key Concept Activity Lab Workbook

e. If the time it took Group Member 1 to walk the path is expressed as the variable t, then express the walking times for the other group members in terms of t. (For example, if Group Member 1 took 5 seconds and Group Member 2 took 4 seconds, then Group Member 1's time is now t and Group Member 2's time is now $t-1$.) Using the formula you found for r in part c, write a rational expression for the speed of each group member in terms of t.

	Variable Expression for Time (in terms of t)	Rational Expression for Speed r (in terms of t, the time for Group Member 1)
Group Member 1	t	$r =$
Group Member 2		$r =$
Group Member 3		$r =$

f. Use your Group Member 1's time and your group's distance to help fill in the chart below.

Situation	Time (seconds)	Speed (meters per second)
June ran three times as fast as the first group member.		
It took Terry 3 seconds longer than the first group member to walk the path.		
Hal was able to run the path in 1/3 the time it took the first group member to walk the path.		

g. Explain what happens to the speed if the time increases but the distance remains the same. What happens to the speed if the time decreases and the distance remains the same.

_____

_____

_____

58   Chapter 6: Rational Expressions Interactive Math—Introductory Algebra

4. Open Environment Activity—Children's Doses of Medicine

Doctors commonly use dose formulas for prescribing medicines to children. These dose formulas describe an approximate relationship only. Young's Rule and Cowling's Rule (two dose formulas) both relate a child's age A in years and an adult dose D of medication to the proper child's dose C. The formulas are most accurate when used for children between the ages of 2 and 13.

Young's Rule: $\quad C = \dfrac{DA}{A+12}$ **Cowling's Rule:** $\quad C = \dfrac{D(A+1)}{24}$

a. Let the adult dose $D = 1000$ mg. Use your spreadsheet tool to create a table which compares the doses predicted by both formulas for children of ages $A = 2, 3, 4, \ldots, 13$.

Age of Child	Child's Dose by Young's Rule	Child's Dose by Cowling's Rule
2		
3		
4		
5		
6		
7		
8		
9		
10		
11		
12		
13		

b. Use the graphing tool to graph the formula for each rule (with $D = 1000$ mg) on the same graph. Record the graphs on the grid below. Pick a scale so that all of the points from the chart will fit on the grid. Label the axes and scales appropriately.

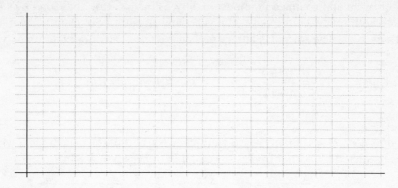

c. Use your table and/or graph to decide whether either formula will consistently predict a larger dose than the other. If one formula does, which one? If not, is there an age at which the doses predicted by one formula become greater than the doses predicted by the other formula? If this is true, estimate that age. Explain your decision.

_____

_____

_____

_____

_____

_____

d. Use the graphing tool and/or the spreadsheet tool to determine if your conclusion in part *c* would be the same if the related adult dose *D* was something other than 1000 mg. Explain how you arrived at your conclusion.

_____

_____

_____

_____

Chapter 7—Further Graphing
Key Concept Activity #7: Chain Reaction

1.   Group Activity—Casting Silver

2.   Conceptual Exercise—How Steep Is This Road?

3.   Extension Exercise—Natural Patterns

4.   Open Environment Activity—Buying Power

1. Group Activity—Casting Silver

After getting her book published, Louise decided to have silver pins designed from the artwork on the book cover. Larry, at Silver Works, told her that the charge for making the casting mold would be $175. Then each pin would cost an additional $25.

a.   Work as a group to fill in the following table to determine the total cost for making different numbers of pins. The first row is done as an example.

Number of Pins	Total Cost for Pins	Arithmetic Set-up and Computations	Ordered Pair (#pins, total cost)
1	$200	$175 + $25(1) = $200	(1 , 200)
2			
3			
4			
5			
6			
7			
8			
9			
10			
n			

b. Use the patterns in the computation column from part *a* to write the formula of the total cost, T, for *n* pins. $T =$ _____

c. In the equation from part *b*, what is the slope of the line? Describe in words what the slope represents.

_____

_____

d. Graph the equation from part *b*, and confirm that the points from the table are on the graph. Pick an appropriate scale to show the graph.

Total Cost, *T*

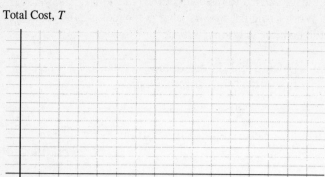

n, Number of Pins Made

e. What is the intercept point of the above graph with the vertical axis? Write both coordinates.

Intercept   (,   )

f. Describe in words what each coordinate of the intercept point from part *e* represents.

g. In your group discuss why the total cost keeps increasing as Louise buys more pins, but the cost per pin decreases and will always be between $25 and $200. Write your summary explanation in the space below. *Hint*, you may want to compute total cost and cost per pin for 1 pin, 10 pins, 200 pins, and so on.

_____

_____

_____

_____

_____

_____

_____

2. Conceptual Exercise—How Steep Is This Road?

Outside of Pendleton, Oregon, a sign warns truck drivers to use low gears because there is a downward grade of 6% for the next 10 miles. *Hint:* A 6% grade is a slope of .06, or a ratio of 6:100. You may need a calculator to complete this exercise.

a. Suppose you start driving at sea level (0 feet altitude) at the bottom of a hill with a 6% upward grade. If it were possible to drive 100 miles (measured horizontally) on this hill with a 6% grade, what would your altitude be after 100 miles? In other words, how high above sea level would you be? Give your answer in miles and then in feet. *Hint:* 1 mile = 5280 feet, so 100 miles = 5280 × 100 feet.

b. If the 10-mile stretch outside of Pendleton were measured horizontally (rather than at an angle), what is the drop in altitude (in feet) within that 10-mile stretch? Show how you arrived at your answer and draw a diagram to illustrate the incline/decline of the road. *Hint:* Convert 10 miles to feet as shown in the hint for part *a*.

c. Denver is called the "Mile High City" because its altitude is approximately 1 mile above sea level. Suppose you are at sea level and Denver is 1000 miles away (measured horizontally). If you are traveling along a highway at a steady incline, what would be the grade of the highway? *Hint:* Convert 1000 miles to feet as shown in part *a*. Use scientific notation and/or a calculator as necessary for computations.

d. Pikes Peak is about 65 miles (measured horizontally) from Denver if you could get there on a straight road with no curves. Pikes Peak has an altitude of about 14,110 ft. If a road could be built from Denver to Pikes Peak with a steady incline and no curves, how steep would the road be? *Hint:* Convert miles to feet. Use a calculator as needed.

e. One route from Denver to Pikes Peak is about 115 miles (measured horizontally). If the incline were the same everywhere on the road, what would be the approximate slope of the road? *Hint:* Use a calculator as needed.

f. Is 1/15 a steep slope? Justify your answer in complete sentences.

_____

_____

_____

_____

_____

_____

3. Extension Exercise—Natural Patterns

Formulas come from observing occurrences or patterns that occur in nature. Many chemical compounds contain natural patterns in molecular arrangement. In this activity, you are to observe some geometric patterns and come up with algebraic formulas that predict what will happen if the patterns continue.

a. The first three cards of a pattern are shown below. Draw circles, squares, and triangles on the next two cards to continue the pattern. Then fill in the chart and determine general formulas to describe the pattern. For each row of the chart, write an ordered pair where the first coordinate is the card number and the second coordinate is the total number of shapes on the card.

Card Number	Number of Squares	Number of Circles	Number of Triangles	Total Number of Shapes	Ordered Pair (Col 1, Col 5)
1					
2					
3					
4					
5					
6					
7					
N					

b. Write the general formula, $f(N)$, for the total number of shapes on the *Nth* card. Use your formula to predict the number of shapes on the following cards:
$f(N) =$ _____ 33 rd card _____ 75th card _____ 150th card _____

c. Plot the ordered pairs from the table above on the grid below. Pick an appropriate window so that all of the points will fit on the grid.

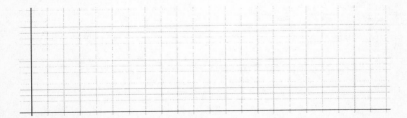

d. Repeat part *a* for the following pattern:

Card Number	Number of Squares	Number of Circles	Number of Triangles	Total Number of Shapes	Ordered Pair (Col 1, Col 5)
1					
2					
3					
4					
5					
6					
7					
N					

e. Write the general formula *f(N)* for the total number of shapes on the *Nth* card. Use your formula to predict the number of shapes on the following cards.

$f(N) = $ _____ 33 rd card _____ 75th card _____ 150th card _____

f. Plot the ordered pairs from the table in part *d* on the grid below. Pick an appropriate scale so that all of the points will fit on the grid.

g. Explain how you can tell whether the function shown in part *f* is linear or not.

_____

_____

_____

_____

4. Open Environment Activity—Buying Power

The table below is a summary of the number of families in the United States and their median income for the years 1970, 1975, 1980, 1985, 1990, and 1995. In 1970, the median income in "current dollars" is shown as $9,867. This means that in 1970, if the incomes of all of the families were listed in numerical order, the income in the middle would have been $9,867. That amount of money in 1970 would have bought a certain number of goods and services. It would have taken $37,485 to buy the same goods and services in 1996. The column, "1996 dollars" gives us a way of comparing the buying power of money across years.

Median Income of Families in the United States

Year	Current dollars	1996 dollars
1970	$9,867	$37,485
1975	13,772	38,449
1980	21,071	40,171
1985	27,843	40,600
1990	35,353	42,440
1995	40,611	41,810

(Source: U. S. Census Bureau)

a. On the grid below, use a black pencil or pen to plot points to show how the median income (current dollars) has changed from 1970 to 1995. In another color, plot points to show how the median income in 1996 dollars has changed from 1970 to 1995.

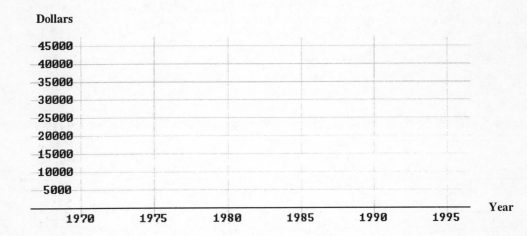

b. Use a straight edge and draw (on the grid in part *a*) a line that approximately goes through the black points that represent median income (current dollars) from 1970 to 1995. Pick two points on the line you drew. Use these points to compute the slope of the line. Use the calculator tool for computations and round the slope to the nearest integer.

  Points: (,   )   (,   )

  Slope ≈ _____

c. In the first column of the spreadsheet tool, enter the years (from the table) and in the second column enter the median income (current dollars). Using the spreadsheet feature, find the equation of a line that approximates the data. Record the resulting function in the space below.

  Median income—in current dollars: $f(x) =$ _____

d. What is the slope of the linear function you got from part *c*? Compare that slope to the one you estimated in part *b*.

e. If the formula in part *c* is used to predict future median income, what would be the projection for the year 2000?

  Projected median income (current dollars): _____

f. Explain why the formula might be valid for short-term projections, but not for long-range projections such as for the year 2050.

_____

_____

_____

_____

_____

Chapter 8—Solving Systems of Linear Equations
Key Concept Activity #8: Check, Please

1.   Open Environment Activity—The Price Is Right

2.   Conceptual Exercise—Comparing Cellular Phone Services

3.   Group Activity—So Many Choices, So Little Time

4.   Extension Exercise—Signing the Best Contract

1. Open Environment Activity—The Price Is Right

Let us consider how the unit price p (in dollars) of some product can affect the quantity that consumers will want to purchase (demand), as well as the quantity that producers are willing to make available to purchase (supply). The supply function, s, is the quantity a producer will supply to the market at different prices p. The demand function, d, is the quantity that consumers will demand at different prices p. Suppose a certain product has the market demand and supply functions given below.

$$d = 2000 - 10p$$
$$s = 5p - 500$$

a. Use the tools in the Open Environment to fill in the quantities supplied and demanded at the given prices in the table below. Explain why the prices from \$0 to \$80 are not valid prices for the supply function.

Price Per Unit (in dollars)	Quantity Demanded	Quantity Supplied
0		
20		
40		
60		
80		
100		
120		
140		
160		
180		
200		

Explanation: _____

_____

_____

_____

_____

b. Explain what the prices $p = \$100$ and $p = \$200$ mean in terms of the problem situation.

A price of $100 means _____

_____

_____

_____

_____

A price of $200 means _____

_____

_____

_____

_____

c. Use the tools in the Open Environment to sketch a graph of the supply and demand functions on the same axes.

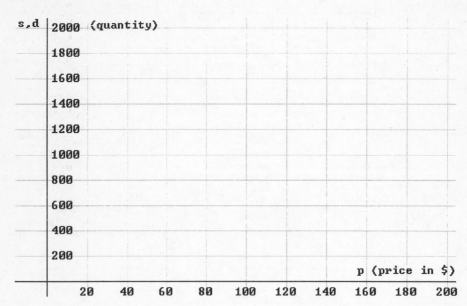

d. Market equilibrium between supply and demand occurs when the quantity supplied equals the quantity demanded. Place a mark on the graph in part *c* where the equilibrium point occurs. Estimate the price and corresponding quantity that produce equilibrium between supply and demand.

Estimated Equilibrium Price: _____ Estimated Equilibrium Quantity: _____

e. Find the answer to part *d* algebraically by substituting the expressions for demand and supply into the equilibrium equation below and then solving the resulting equation for price *p*. Record the price to the nearest penny. What quantity will be produced at this price? Round this quantity to the nearest unit.

$$\text{Supply} = \text{Demand}$$

Price: _____   Quantity: _____

f. At a price of $180, what quantity is the producer willing to supply? How much will consumers be willing to purchase? Explain using complete sentences.

_____

_____

_____

_____

_____

_____

_____

_____

g. In general, how do you think the market will react to a price above equilibrium?

_____

_____

_____

_____

_____

_____

_____

_____

_____

_____

2. •Conceptual Exercise—Comparing Cellular Phone Services

The cost of subscribing to cellular phone services can differ widely depending on which cellular service carrier you choose. The total monthly cost depends on a monthly access charge, which is a fixed fee to provide and sustain your account, and airtime charges for time to make and receive calls. The airtime charges include when you call (peak or off-peak time) and where you call from (home or "roam").

The table below shows the price of the lowest service rate plans for different cellular service carriers in the Dallas/Fort Worth area. The two numbers under "Home" represent peak time/off-peak time rates when calling from the home area.

Cellular Service Carrier	Monthly Access Charge ($)	Free Airtime Included (in minutes)	Charges/minute (¢)	
			Home	Roam
AT&T Wireless	29.99	30	49/49¢	49¢
PrimeCo	27.00	0	27/27	27
Southwestern Bell	26.95	15	48/50	50
MCI	45.95	45	32/06	59

(source: Consumer Reports, February 1997)

a. Notice that for AT&T Wireless and PrimeCo, the charge per minute for airtime is the same during peak time at home, off-peak time at home, and roam time. What is the constant rate for airtime, in dollars per minute, for the first two carriers?

　　　AT&T Wireless airtime rate: _____　　　PrimeCo airtime rate: _____

b. When determining your total monthly cost, what is the independent variable or input?

_____

c. When determining your total monthly cost, what is the dependent variable or output?

_____

d. Describe the independent and dependent variables in symbolic terms.

e. What is the constant monthly access charge (fixed cost) for each carrier?

　　　AT&T Wireless:_____　　　PrimeCo: _____

f. Assuming that all customers talk for 30 minutes or more, write a variable expression that
   represents the monthly cost for airtime (variable cost)? *Hint:* For AT&T Wireless, you need
   to account for the first 30 minutes being free.

   AT&T Wireless: _____   PrimeCo: _____

g. Combine the constant from part *e* and the variable expression from part *f* to obtain an
   equation giving total monthly cost (in dollars) for each carrier in terms of airtime (in
   minutes.)

   AT&T Wireless: PrimeCo:

h. Consider the equations found in part *g* to be a system of two equations in two variables.
   Complete the table of values below.

Airtime (in minutes)	AT&T Wireless Cost ($)	PrimeCo Cost ($)
30		
35		
40		
45		
50		
55		
60		
65		
70		
75		

2. **Conceptual Exercise—Comparing Cellular Phone Services**   **Key Concept Activity #8: Check, Please**

i. State when each carrier is the most economical to use and explain your reasoning.

_____

_____

_____

_____

_____

j. Graph the system of equations over the time interval from 30 minutes to 75 minutes. Use different colors for the different carriers. Estimate the amount of airtime for which both carriers have equal total monthly costs.

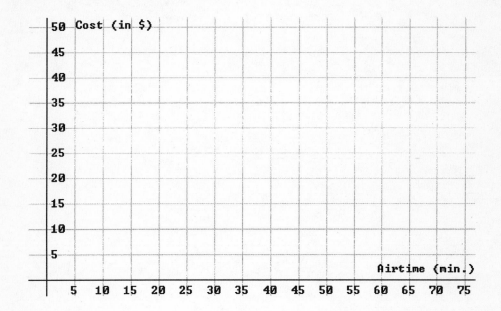

What is the approximate amount of airtime for which both carriers have the same total montly costs? Round your result to the nearest whole minute. _____

k. Now consider the first 30 minutes of airtime. On the coordinate plane in part *j,* plot the cost function for airtime from 0 minutes to 30 minutes for AT&T Wireless and then do the same for PrimeCo. Use different colors to make this time interval distinct. *Hint:* Recall that AT&T gives the first 30 minutes of airtime at no extra cost.

3. Group Activity—So Many Choices, So Little Time

In the last exercise, if x represents the amount of airtime (in minutes) and y the total monthly cost (in dollars) for using a cellular phone, then the problem can be modeled by the following system of equations.

$$\text{AT \& T Wireless}: \quad y = 0.49(x - 30) + 29.99, \text{ where } x \geq 30$$
$$\text{PrimeCo}: \qquad\qquad y = 0.27x + 27$$

a. Find the exact amount of airtime (to the nearest minute) for which both carriers have the same total monthly cost. As a group, decide whether to solve the system of equations by the substitution method or the addition method. Give reasons for this choice.

Solution Process:

Reasoning: _____

_____

_____

b. Now your group is to consider all four carriers listed in the table from the last exercise. Your job is to write a letter to all consumers in the Dallas/Fort Worth area explaining how they should go about choosing the most economical carrier. In the space below, include any tables, graphs, or algebra necessary to support your written analysis, which should be completed on the next page.

Written Analysis to Consumers

_____

_____

_____

_____

_____

_____

_____

_____

_____

_____

_____

_____

_____

_____

_____

_____

_____

4. Extension Exercise—Signing the Best Contract

Suppose that Megan wrote a romance novel during her last year in school, and two publishers extend her offers to sign the manuscript for publication. Company A offers her a $10,000 sign-on bonus and 15% of the book's total sales. Company B offers her a $5,000 sign-on bonus and 18% of the book's total sales. Assuming both companies would spend about the same amount on advertising and promoting the book, which publisher should she sign with?

a. Construct a table that shows Megan's book income as a function of total sales.

Total Sales ($)	Income from Company A ($)	Income from Company B ($)
$0		
25,000		
50,000		
75,000		
100,000		
125,000		
150,000		
175,000		
200,000		

b. Describe the patterns in the incomes from Companies A and B as total sales increase.

_____

_____

_____

c. Plot the income from Company A as a function of sales, connect the points with a straight line, and label it A. On the same graph, plot the income from Company B as a function of sales, connect the points with a straight line, and label it B.

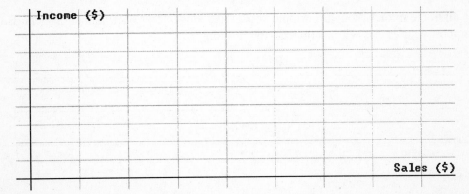

d. Let x be the total sales (in dollars) and y be the income (in dollars) that Megan would receive. Using these variables, set up a system of equations for the incomes from Companies A and B. Then solve the system using the substitution method.

Company A:

Company B:

e. Explain what the solution to the system means in terms of the problem situation.

_____

_____

_____

f. Explain the meaning of the slope and y-intercept in each equation in terms of the problem situation.

_____

_____

_____

g. Based on all of the information, how would you advise Megan on selecting a publisher? Be sure to support your advice with mathematical reasoning.

_____

_____

_____

_____

Chapter 9—Roots and Radicals
Key Concept Activity #9: Mysteries of the Past

1.   Conceptual Exercise—The Shortest Distance Between Two Points

2.   Open Environment Activity—Sight Depends on Height

3.   Extension Exercise—Amateur Archaeologist

4.   Group Activity—Seeing Is Believing

1. Conceptual Exercise—The Shortest Distance Between Two Points

Currently, the only way to get from Center City to Pythagorean Airport is to travel 10 miles along Euclid Expressway, make a 90° turn onto Fermat Freeway, and go another 15 miles before reaching the airport. Because of traffic, the average speed along Euclid Expressway is 45 mph, and the average speed along Fermat Freeway is 40 mph. This produces a travel time that discourages many businesses from locating in Center City. A new route called Hypotenuse Highway has been proposed to connect Center City directly to the airport in a straight line. As part of the construction project team, you have been asked to complete the following tasks.

a. Draw a diagram (with labels) which illustrates the situation described above.

b. Find the distance from Center City to Pythagorean Airport via the proposed Hypotenuse Highway route. Round your answer to the nearest whole mile.

c. If an average speed of 65 mph can be expected when traveling along Hypotenuse Highway, what is the average time of travel between Center City and Pythagorean Airport? Round your answer to the nearest tenth of an hour. Then convert the time to the nearest minute.

d. Find the time it currently takes to travel along the existing right angle route. Round your answer to the nearest tenth of an hour. Then convert the time to the nearest minute.

e. Approximately how many minutes will the new route save the average traveler?

f. What are some other factors to consider before going ahead with the project?

_____

_____

_____

_____

_____

_____

2.   Open Environment Activity—Sight Depends on Height

The viewing distance (in miles) from a height (in feet) above the earth's surface can be estimated by the following function.

$$d = 1.225\sqrt{h}$$

One of the most famous tall buildings in the United States is the Empire State Building in New York City. The building is 1250 feet tall, and if you include the 164-foot TV tower at the top, its total height is 1414 feet.

a.   Using the distance function above, how far can you see from the top of the building if you are looking out toward the horizon? Round your answer to the nearest tenth of a mile.

b.   List some conditions under which the function might not give accurate results.

_____

_____

_____

_____

c.   Assuming that the TV tower is able to transmit a signal in a straight line toward the horizon, what is the maximum distance that the signal can travel? Round your answer to the nearest tenth of a mile.

d.   Use the tools in the Open Environment to create a table that shows the relationship between height and viewing distance toward the horizon. Round distances to the nearest tenth of a mile.

Height, h (in feet)	Distance, d (in miles)
0	
200	
400	
600	
800	
1000	
1200	
1400	
1600	
1800	

e. Use the Open Environment to create a graph of the viewing distance as a function of height above the earth's surface.

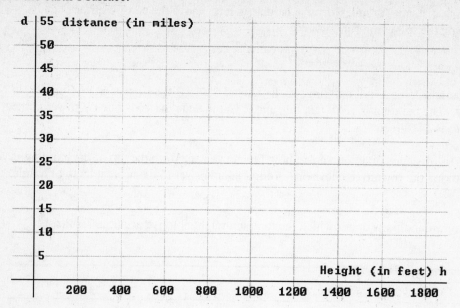

f. Use complete sentences to describe how height affects viewing distance over the interval of 0 feet to 1800 feet.

_____

_____

_____

_____

_____

3. Extension Exercise—Amateur Archaeologist

In Key Concept Activity #9: Mysteries of the Past, pieces of a Mayan stele were found at the site you mapped. Suppose that Dr. Drybones also found a piece of broken pottery and has traced the inside curve of an excavated fragment called a rim sherd. He wants to use this curve to find the circumference of the pot's opening. Dr. Drybones has completed the first four steps, given below, and wants you to continue the process of finding the circumference.

I.   Draw a straight line that connects two points on the curve and label its length C. This line is called a chord.

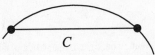

II. Find the midpoint of the chord and from this point measure the middle ordinate distance, M, by drawing the perpendicular distance to the curve.

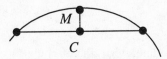

III Redraw the figure to include the unknown radius, R, so that there is a right triangle to which we can apply the Pythagorean theorem.

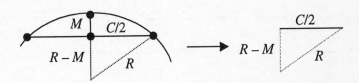

IV. Using the Pythagorean theorem, $a^2 + b^2 = c^2$, we obtain the formula below.

$$\left(\frac{C}{2}\right)^2 + (R - M)^2 = R^2$$

a. Show the algebraic work that needs to be completed on the formula in Step IV to isolate R and obtain the radius formula given below.

$$R = \frac{C^2}{8M} + \frac{M}{2}$$

b. Go to step II and use a metric ruler to measure the length C of the chord and middle ordinate distance M in centimeters. Record your results below.

Length of chord $C =$ _____   Middle ordinate distance $M =$ _____

c. Calculate the radius R in centimeters by substituting the values of C and M into the radius formula given in part *a*. Round your answer to the hundredths place.

Radius $R =$ _____

d. Use the radius found in part *c* to calculate the circumference of the opening in centimeters, where $Circumference = 2\pi R$. Round your answer to the hundredths place.

Circumference = _____

e. Based on the size of the vessel's opening, what do you think this pottery vessel was used for? Why would data on a pottery vessel's size, shape, and volume be important to archaeologists looking for clues to the past? Answer in complete sentences and support your answer with logical reasoning.

_____

_____

_____

_____

_____

_____

4. Group Activity—Seeing Is Believing

In the Open Environment Activity—Sight Depends on Height, you were given the function,

$$d = 1.225\sqrt{h}$$

This equation approximates the viewing distance d (in miles) from a height h (in feet) above the earth's surface. But where did this formula come from and why does it work? Let's investigate!

Suppose you want to know how far you can see from the top of Mt. Rainier, located in the state of Washington, with an elevation of 14,410 feet or about 2.7 miles. Using the radius of the earth which is about 3960 miles, we construct a right triangle below (not to scale) whose legs are the earth's radius and an unknown line of sight, d, and whose hypotenuse is the radius plus the height of Mt. Rainier. Note: d is a distance along a tangent line, it must be perpendicular to the radius of the circle representing the earth.

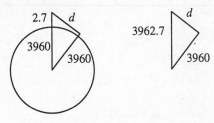

a. Working with your group members, use the Pythagorean theorem ($leg^2 + leg^2 = hypotenuse^2$) to obtain an equation based on the sides of the right triangle. Then solve the equation for d.

b. Substitute Mt Rainier's elevation (in feet) into the original viewing distance function (at the top of the page) and simplify to see if you obtain about the same answer as in part a.

c. Suppose h is the height in miles from the surface of the earth to the top of some object, such as Mt. Rainier. Use the Pythagorean theorem to obtain an equation based on the sides of the right triangle below. Then show the algebra needed to write d as a function of h to obtain,

$d = \sqrt{h^2 + 7920h}$.

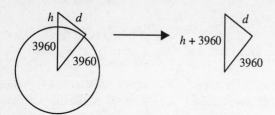

d. The expression under the radical in part c has two terms, but since h^2 is very small relative to 7290h, perhaps we could ignore the first term without loosing much accuracy in approximating the viewing distance d. Complete the table below to find out.

h (miles)	$d = \sqrt{h^2 + 7920h}$ (miles)	$d = \sqrt{7920h}$ (miles)
1		
5		
10		
25		
50		

Does it seem reasonable to use the third column formula to calculate viewing distance? Explain your answer using complete sentences.

_____

_____

_____

_____

e. Write a function equivalent to $d = \sqrt{7920h}$ that allows you to input the height in feet instead of miles. Hint: 1 mile = 5280 feet.

f. Now, show how you can obtain $d = 1.225\sqrt{h}$ (where d is in miles and h is in feet) from the function you developed in part e.

Chapter 10—Solving Quadratic Equations
Key Concept Activity #10: Reaching the Peak

1.   Extension Exercise—Maximum Profit at the Mountain Bike Shop

2.   Open Environment Activity—What Goes Up Must Come Down

3.   Conceptual Exercise—Supply and Demand for In-Line Skates

4.   Group Activity—Speed and Stopping Distances

1. Extension Exercise—Maximum Profit at the Mountain Bike Shop

In Key Concept Activity #10: Reaching the Peak, our goal was to find the price p (in dollars) that generated the greatest possible revenue R (in dollars). The market research data for adult bikes, shown below, gave the relationship between price and number of hourly rentals per day d (rental demand). Now consider the cost of operating the business. Suppose all daily costs are fixed at $355, except for the maintenance of the bikes, which is $2 per number of hourly rentals.

a. Using the data in the first two columns, complete the following table.

Hourly Price p	Number of Hourly Rentals Per Day d	Daily Revenue R	Daily Operating Cost C	Daily Profit $R - C$
$6.00	225			
$7.00	200			
$8.00	165			
$9.00	120			

b. Based on the data above, estimate the price you think the bike shop should set for the hourly rental of an adult bike. Explain your reasoning.

_____

_____

_____

_____

_____

c. A computer or graphing calculator can be used to find an equation that best fits the above data for price p and demand d. This equation, called a demand equation, is

$$d = -35p + 440.$$

Find a formula for the cost C as a function of the price p by substituting the expression for demand d into the model below and then simplifying it.

$$C = 2 \bullet d + 355$$

Revenue is the product of hourly price p and the number of hourly rentals or demand d.

$$R = p \bullet d$$

$$R = p \bullet (-35p + 440)$$

$$R = -35p^2 + 440p$$

d. Use the economic principle below to find a formula for the daily profit as a function of price. To do so, substitute the expression for R (revenue) given above and the expression for C (cost) from part c. Write the profit function in simplest form by combining like terms.

$$\text{Profit} = \text{Revenue} - \text{Cost}$$

e. Use the profit function developed in part d to complete the table below.

Price	$6.00	$6.50	$7.00	$7.50	$8.00	$8.50	$9.00
Profit							

f. Based on this table, what price would you set for the hourly rental of adult bikes? Explain.

_____

_____

_____

g. Look back at the table in part a, and explain why the profits for hourly prices of $6, $7, $8, or $9 are different from those in the table in part e.

_____

_____

_____

_____

h. Graph the profit function in part *d* over the interval [2, 10] including the data points from part *e*. Then connecting the points with a smooth curve. What is the name of a graph with this shape?

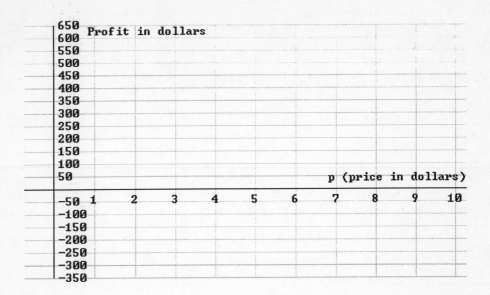

i. Mark the point on the graph where the bike shop first breaks even on adult bike rentals and and label it "BE". Estimate to the nearest dollar the coordinates of the ordered pair that corresponds to the break-even point.

Estimate of break-even point: (_____, _____)

j. Find the price (to the nearest cent) at which the bike shop breaks even by setting the profit function in part *d* equal to zero and then solving the resulting quadratic equation. Explain why this price is important to the bike shop.

_____

_____

_____

k. Mark the point on the graph where the bike shop makes the greatest profit on adult bike rentals and label it "MP". Estimate to the nearest dollar the coordinates of the ordered pair that corresponds to this point.

Estimate of maximum profit point: (_____ , _____)

l. Find the exact price that produces the maximum profit for the function developed in part *d* by using the fact that the vertex of the parabola $y = ax^2 + bx + c$ has x-coordinate $-b/2a$. Round the price and the maximum profit obtained at this price to the nearest cent.

Maximum profit: _____   Price to charge: _____

m. Describe in complete sentences how profit changes as price increases from $6.00 to $9.00. Include what price you would charge and the reasons why.

_____

_____

_____

_____

_____

2. Open Environment Activity—What Goes Up Must Come Down

Suppose a soccer player kicks a ball and its height, h, in feet, after t seconds is given by the following quadratic function:

$$h = -16t^2 + 80t \quad \text{(first kick)}.$$

a. Use the Open Environment to construct a table of values that shows the height of the ball (first kick) every half second during the first six seconds. (Leave the third column blank for now.)

Time (seconds) t	Height h (feet)	
	First Kick	**Second Kick**
0		
0.5		
1		
1.5		
2		
2.5		
3		
3.5		
4		
4.5		
5		

b. Use the data from the first two columns to find when the first kicked ball reaches its maximum height. Explain your answer using complete sentences.

_____

_____

c. Sketch a graph of the above data and connect the points with a smooth curve. Label the point where the maximum height occurs with its corresponding ordered pair.

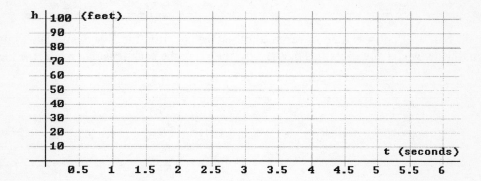

d. Now suppose the same player makes a second kick of the ball when it is already 1 foot off the ground. The quadratic function that models the height of the ball as a function of time is given below. Use the Open Environment to fill in the third column of the table on the previous page.

$$h = -16t^2 + 70t + 1$$

e. Use the Open Environment to construct a graph of the second kick, showing height h as a function of time t over the interval from $t = 0$ to $t = 4.5$ seconds. Sketch the graph on the previous page on the same set of coordinate axes used for the graph of the first kick.

f. Use the trace feature of your graphing tool to help approximate the maximum height. Find and label this point on the graph.

g. When does the ball from the second kick hit the ground? To determine this, first get an approximate solution by using the trace feature on your grapher. Then use the quadratic formula to verify your approximation. Show all work and round your solution to the nearest tenth of a second.

h. Use complete sentences to describe how the heights from the first and second kicks compare from time 0 to 5 seconds.

_____

_____

_____

_____

i. Explain how the ball was able to reach a greater height from the first kick than from the second. How would you know this fact just by observing the equations that model the kicks?

_____

_____

_____

3. **Conceptual Exercise—Supply and Demand for In-Line Skates**

Suppose that in addition to renting in-line skates, the Mountain Bike Shop starts selling them. The managers want to sell just one model that is known to be popular. They conduct a survey of consumers to determine how many of them would buy the skates at different prices. The managers also survey suppliers of that model of skates to determine what quantities they would provide to the bike shop at different prices. The survey results are given in the table below.

Market Price	Number of Skates	
	Demand	Supply
$80	225	20
$85	160	30
$90	110	60
$95	75	110
$100	55	180

a. Graph the data in the first two columns with price as the independent variable and the number of skates demanded by consumers as the dependent variable. Connect these points with a smooth curve and label it *d*, the demand curve. Then graph the data in the first and third columns with price as the independent variable and the number of skates suppliers are willing to provide as the dependent variable. Connect these points with a smooth curve and label it *s*, the supply curve.

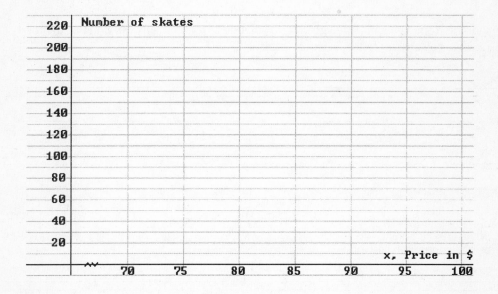

b. Estimate the market price at which the number of skates demanded by consumers equals the number of skates that suppliers are willing to provide. The price at which supply equals demand is the market equilibrium point.

c. The relationship between price and demand can be modeled by a quadratic function and so can the relationship between price and supply. The equations showing demand d as a function of price x and supply s as a function of price x are given below. These equations only make sense for prices between $80 and $100.

$$d = 0.2x^2 - 43x + 2360 \quad \text{and} \quad s = 0.4x^2 - 64x + 2580$$

Substitute the demand and supply expressions into the equilibrium equation below. Rearrange the terms of the equation so that it is in standard form ($ax^2 + bx + c = 0$). Then use the quadratic formula to find the selling price that produces market equilibrium.

Demand = Supply

d. The quadratic formula should have given two solutions. Explain why only one of them makes sense as an answer to the question in part *c.*

_____

_____

_____

_____

e. As the price increases from $80 to $100, the demand curve decreases (goes down from left to right) and the supply curve increases (goes up from left to right). Explain why this happens in terms of the problem situation.

_____

_____

_____

4. Group Activity—Speed and Stopping Distances

Suppose that while driving you see the brake lights of the car in front of you come on. If you assume the car ahead is going to stop and that your brakes must be applied, then how far will your car travel before it comes to a complete stop? In other words, what is the stopping distance from the moment your brain receives the signal to stop until the car is no longer moving?

The table below contains data on this situation. Note that the total stopping distance is the sum of the reaction distance (the distance traveled from the time you realize that you must brake until your foot hits the brake pedal) and the braking distance (distance traveled after the brakes are pressed).

Speed (km/hr)	Reaction Distance (meters)	Braking Distance (meters)	Total Stopping Distance (meters)
10	2	2	4
20	4	3	7
30	6	6	12
40	8	10	18
50	10	15	25
60	12	22	34
70	14	29	43
80	16	38	54
90	18	48	66
100	20	60	80
110	22	73	95

(Source: Traffic Board of Western Australia)

a. Notice the pattern in the first two columns and find an equation that gives the reaction distance R (in meters) as a function of the speed x (in kilometers per hour).

b. The model for braking distance B (in meters) as a function of the speed x (in kilometers per hour) is $B = 0.00635x^2 - 0.05406x + 1.84$. Use this equation and the equation from part *a* to find an equation for total stopping distance y (in meters), as a function of the speed x (in kilometers per hour). Write the equation for total stopping distance in simplest form by combining like terms.

c. Use the total stopping distance equation just developed to generate a table of (x, y) data pairs. Approximate the stopping distance y to the nearest meter. Remember that these values are from the model you developed and will not exactly match the real data in the previous table.

Speed x (km/hr)	10	20	30	40	50	60	70	80	90	100	110
Stopping Distance y (m)											

d. Compare the data in the table above with the original data from the first and fourth columns of the table on the previous page. Does your equation for total stopping distance accurately model the real data for this situation? Use complete sentences to explain your answer.

_____

_____

_____

e. Use a rectangular coordinate system to graph the points from your (x, y) table and connect the points with a smooth curve.

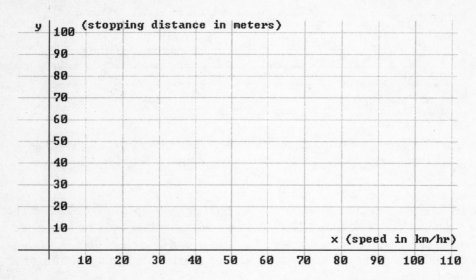

f. Explain the relationship between speed and stopping distance as speed increases.

_____

_____

_____